A STORY BEYOND DIMENSIONS

OF MANY JOURNEYS TOGETHER

MUSIC

Copyright © Music
All Rights Reserved.

This book is being dedicated for my special person and the love of my life. I will cherish you with all my heart and love. I hope you like my work of art. Thank you so much for being with me and for the coming years as our relationship to strenghten more and may we live a happy, healthy and prosperous life.

For my readers, Kindly shower your blessings for the both of us to be together forever. I hope you all would like my poetry which was made at random times as in times of good and bad.

Once again, I dedicate this for the love of my life. Be with me forever.

Contents

Preface

The Book which I wrote began when the pandemic started and started to realize more on emotional feelings of humans and to write in a short way to reach out to my readers. Thus, writing of this book started and many more are in the way for giving my readers a time for them to realize and to understand how simple life is.

Your feedback is my treasure and a motivator for me to write more upcoming projects for the future. Thank you in advance for your support.

With Love,

Music.

1. THE TIME MACHINE

Oh Here, Oh Hear,
The tale of time and rampant woes,
Oh where, Oh there,
Tears of sorrow and of hope.
Wish of mine, as a small one,
Wants to go, go to the past;
Wander around farther there,
Waterfall, mountains over and near.
Atlast to find me, the small weak me,
To give a hand, to cross the bridge,
As me, the little one ,scared and alone,
"Hey me, I came to comfort thee."

2. BREAKDOWN/ CHAPTER OF LOWEST POINT

Peace in me, in shambles, tearing me apart,
Ever as always a loner, yet crumble of joy exists,
And stand in the dark, light no more inside; as
Creeps and haunts me, wants to destroy within,
Evolving of the past as wants to corrupt my light.
Period of time came, for being low and lower,
Entail a track, keeps the joy in locks, vaccums
Au revior to all, as starts the battle for thy for,
Cramped up, sealed up, locked up, yearning that
End comes, as I hit the lowest point, Breadown begins.

3. Life in the Concrete Jungle

Life as we know, dust breaks; dawn rise,
In the mist of dust, dirt and debris, killing
The insides and out, starts the journey of,
Concrete here and traffic there, happy or grim;
Jungle safari as the travel goes, a daily life it is.

4. Disenchantment

To many may seem, in life as it comes,
Rustling upon the waters of time and ire,
Used to say, to worth upon, when change comes;
Such distress as it was and were, a downward fall,
To say that to, be self and to ignore the falling empire.

5. Out of the common

Reach out to the stars, Come out of the woods, many say,
Affinity as it seems, some are pelting hate and hatred;
Rise to the occassion and yet, we dwell in dreams, to be free,
Enigma of being the real me, as out of the common to be.

6. Fake Smile

Fall for it, as good as it looks, ghosting around,
Avail of confidence, a sign of sheer love and acceptance;
Knowing of surrender as truthful to be, aware of
Eclipstic behaviour as failure to note; a fake smile.

7. Dilemma

Stuck in the whirlwind, of wrong and right; glitters
In the limelight as red or blue, the road to go too,
The harbouring effect as glee, muddled in covers,
Middle of who is who and what for? The Dilemma!!

8. Happy to be a Loner

Laugh and play for self, as thyself is strong, elegant, pure,
Obsessed with blues, cheering and styling for self, self care,
Never to be, with others, with specials as it fades soon as;
Ever be, for you, with you, celebrate each moment,
Reach out to the skies above, me as the moon strong and mighty.

9. Lost

Love all day, love all night, love is love for all,
Out of reach, of many or few, yet looking for you;
Simple yet complex, simile yet metaphor, still confused,
Truce yet vile, searching for the lost in me.

10. Words

Just simple and complex are they, like Pumice for thoughts,
Yet tone of many, changes all, creeps all, confuses all, all for all,
As sweet as it gets, and teary as it makes, uncomfy and cool;
Quivering for some, so hurtful, so cruel, so not into the realm.
For these are just, as they say, the power lies within,
Them, these, they, who say, who hears, hate and nice,
To the start, to the end, to the love, to the foe, makes all, One;
Sharpen or blunt, the mighty of words to be uttered from thee.

11. 13 to 26

The day of horror starts, as the skies are grey,
Hope for goodness, went to the drain of lost souls,
Fades beyond, prescribed limits, walking into the dark,
Away and beyond, wandering for love and to be cared for.
The suffers still lasting, scars were made, not forgotten;
Abyss of fears, falsehood, flattery, flew across me,
Of many, claimed my realness, true self, openness, agile,
Calamitous going on, as from 13 to 26 and till where ??
Where??.....

12. 2 Mister

The one being a dreamer, The other being a leader,
Cross paths led to one other, starts the helm of life,
Choices shatter, likes collide, makes them unique and
Separated from, say all, say many, but both are one to one.
One day came, One day flew, actions speak and both are for one,
Days passed, as they grew stronger, stronger as they grew,
Omnificient;
Yet the test of time clouded, upon them, show of love and care,
Eventually crossed, but the humans differ, to live in and what
they did ????...
......To be continued.

13. The Essence of me

I love me as I love me more, the true self inside sheds,
Say selenophile, adore and love into, Melophile, Music;
Heart of pluviophile, crazy and let go, mixed from many,
Amicable always, whisper lover, as it continues, Change.

14. Feliz Cumpleaños

Happy returns, happy day, a special day for you,
Always be blessed, with prosperity, lots of joy,
Special are you, for all of us, passionate in work you do;
Enthusiastic, always a doer, creative at its finest,
Enthralled by many, as you, with a good heart,
Birthday for you, Happy Birthday to you.

15. Birthday Note

Sum of all the love you gave, for all the Work

All your care, as I won't say adieu,

Thank you for all, as my heart bloom

Healthy as many years to come, my papa

I wish for you, greatness and happier

Say for you, my dear father

Happy Birthday to you, my dear appa.

16. Congratulations

Perfect as always. you be you,
Rise and above, from meanies
And many years of it, teased upon;
Versions of you, hard to defeat,
In with a big heart, a heart of love,
Never fear for, as happy for you thee.

The End Of First Book

The Joy in me, when I wrote this book and I hope my readers would also love reading this book. A Kind request to all is that to wirte a poem in your style. Use this space to write your lovable work of art.

Thank you once again for spending your time to read my work and I hope you will feel yourself and to empower yourself.

Thank you.